THE NEW MAP
OF THE GLOBAL
CHURCH

THE NEW MAP
OF THE
GLOBAL CHURCH

PHILIP JENKINS

A Crossroad Book
The Crossroad Publishing Company

The Crossroad Publishing Company
www.CrossroadPublishing.com
© 2017 by Philip Jenkins

In continuation of our 200-year tradition of independent publishing, The Crossroad Publishing Company proudly offers a variety
of books with strong, original voices and diverse perspectives. The
viewpoints expressed in our books are not necessarily those of
The Crossroad Publishing Company, any of its imprints or of its
employees, executives, owners. Although the author and publisher
have made every effort to ensure that the information in this book
was correct at press time, the author and publisher do not assume
and hereby disclaim any liability to any party for any loss, dam-
age, or disruption caused by errors or omissions, whether such
errors or omissions result from negligence, accident, or any other
cause. No claims are made or responsibility assumed for any health
or other benefits.

Book design by The HK Scriptorium

Library of Congress Cataloging-in-Publication Data
available from the Library of Congress.

ISBN 978-0-8245-2078-6

Books published by The Crossroad Publishing Company may be
purchased at special quantity discount rates for classes and insti-
tutional use. For information, please e-mail sales@Crossroad
Publishing.com.

ISBN 978-0-8245-5009-7 (epub)

CONTENTS

Contents

INTRODUCTION

A century ago, the vast majority of the world's Christians—over 80 percent—lived in Europe and North America. In our lifetimes, that distribution has been changing very rapidly, so that by 2050, the faith will find its largest concentrations in the Global South, in Africa, Asia, and Latin America. By that date, Africa alone will be the largest Christian continent, containing a third of all believers. We are presently living through one of the greatest revolutions in the story of the faith.

Scholars sometimes speak of the rise of a "Global" Christianity as if that is a new or experimental phenomenon, but in reality it is anything but that. Of its nature, Christianity must be a worldwide faith, which carries its message to all cultures, all peoples and races:

it must be global. It falls short of this ideal if it identifies itself with any one race or region, if it defines itself as European or American, or even African. How can such a faith limit itself to any one continent or nation or city? If it is not global, surely it is not Christianity.

Yet it is so easy to forget the faith's global quality. For several centuries, we have been accustomed to think of Christianity as the distinctive tradition of Europe, and of Europe's outlying territories and former colonies, especially in the Americas. In 1920, Anglo-French Catholic writer Hilaire Belloc boasted that "Europe is the faith, and the faith is Europe."

But historically, that statement was far from true. Christianity, of course, began in the Middle East, and developed its beliefs and structures in countries such as Syria, Palestine, and Egypt. That Middle Eastern presence remained long after the Muslim conquests of those regions. Even a thousand years ago, at the midpoint of the faith's history, Christianity was transcontinental, with thriving centers in Africa and Asia as well as Europe. Ancient churches flourished in Syria, Iraq, and Ethiopia, and more Christians probably lived in Asia than Europe.

Only in the fourteenth and fifteenth centuries were many of these populations destroyed through war, persecution, and forced conversions. This was also the time when Europe itself was finally Christianized, with the conversion of the once-mighty pagan kingdom of Lithuania. Only around 1450 did Christianity worldwide assume what we today assume to be its natural form, as "the faith of Europe."

Christianity did indeed become "European," but about a millennium later than most people think.

This history tells us much about the faith's cultural dimensions. Although we may assume that Christianity is intimately linked to particular kinds of art, architecture, or literature, that is not necessarily so. Culturally, as well as geographically, Christianity has no heart, no natural core. Of course, it began in Palestine, in the Holy Land, but only rarely have Christians held power over that territory during the past thirteen centuries. The faith's original homeland—the region where it enjoyed its greatest triumphs over its first millennium—is now overwhelmingly Muslim.

This lack of a heartland is in stark contrast to the history of Islam, which originated in Arabia and neighboring lands, and has always continued to find its heart there. From that solid base, Islam has spread over large sections of Asia and Africa, occasionally losing some territories, such as Spain and the Balkans, but always retaining its heartland, and speaking its Arabic language. The Christian center of gravity, on the other hand, has shifted over time. For long centuries, the faith found its most active centers in the Near East, but in later eras, the cultural and demographic heart of the church moved west, and later south. That center moves daily closer to the equator.

We are wrong, then, if we ever think of the faith as something that belongs naturally in one part of the world, whatever that may be, and which must be carried to other regions on the edges, the periphery. Historically, all lands that became Christian were once on the periphery of the church, and in future years they might be so once again. As the great historian Leopold von Ranke famously proclaimed, "All ages are equidistant from eternity, and just as immediately accessible to God's presence." And so are all lands.

No earthly place can claim to be the heart of Christianity. We all stand at the periphery, and must act accordingly. A local church that I know has a signboard that expresses this truth well. As worshipers drive out of the car park, they read the words "You are now entering the mission field."

Christianity, then, is linked to no one place, but rather to all places. Its only home is the church. As we read in the Epistle to the Hebrews, "here we do not have an enduring city, but we are looking for the city that is to come."

1

RELIGION BY THE NUMBERS
Demography Drives Changes

Demography drives religious change. That bald comment is too obvious to be worth making, but it's surprising how little attention demographic factors receive in most histories of religion, particularly of Christianity. That neglect means we miss a very large part of the story.

Given a sufficiently high birth rate, a minority religious community can rapidly become a dominant majority, with all that implies for distributing social power and shaping conflict. Alternatively, migration can transform the religious economy of a hitherto static society.

Demographics also shape the prevailing forms of religion. A country with a marked youth bulge—with lots of adolescents and young adults—is far more open to explosive revivalism than a more sedate and middle-aged society. Changing demographics can also have a pastoral impact, revolutionizing perceptions of childhood and old age. Numbers may not be everything, but they certainly are something.

Also in the category of "what everyone knows" is the fact that Christian numbers are growing in Africa and elsewhere while they are stable or shrinking in Europe. What we miss in such a simple statement is the sheer scale of the demographic change, quite apart from any religious concerns. The global shift in populations represents one of the most significant facts of our time. And unlike religious changes, which are subject to so many qualifications about what we can and cannot know, the demographic story rests on quite solid quantitative foundations.

Take the continent of Africa. In 1900, Africa had around 100 million people, or 6 percent of the global population. In 2005, the number of Africans reached 1 billion, or 15 percent of humanity. By 2050, Africa's population will be between 2 billion and 2.25 billion, which will then be about a quarter of the world's people. Those numbers do not count African migrants in Europe and North America.

Population growth comes into even sharper focus when seen in a local context. By contemporary standards, just a century ago, human beings were sparsely distributed across large stretches of Africa. In 1900, the parts of East Africa that would become Kenya, Uganda, and Tanzania were occupied by just 7 or 8 million people, in an area not much smaller than Western Europe. By 2000, the three countries had a combined population of 90 million. By 2050, they might have 260 million. Growth in West Africa was almost as staggering. In 1900, the lands that would become Nigeria had around 16 million people, rising to 160 million today and probably to around 300 million by 2050.

Now let's set those numbers alongside those for Europe. In 1900 there were 400 million Europeans, a number that rose to 730 million today. But in relative terms, as a share of global population, Europe was in steep decline. Europeans made up a quarter of humanity in 1900, as against 11 percent today; and it is projected to fall to 8 percent by 2050. In 1900, Europeans outnumbered Africans by four to one. By 2050, Africans should have a three to one advantage over Europeans.

That global revolution echoes through every aspect of life, through all social and economic structures. For one thing, all those new Africans have to find somewhere to live, so Africa in coming decades will be experiencing the greatest wave of urbanization in human history. This fact has incalculable consequences for political stability and quite possibly for international tensions. Moreover, different parts of the world are marked by radically different proportions of young and old. Of the ten nations with the highest population growth rates, all but one are in Africa. All the nations experiencing population decline are in Europe, with the exception of Japan.

These numbers have major religious consequences, and not just for Christianity. In coming decades, the non-Arab share of Islam will continue to grow, with a far larger proportion of Muslims coming from Africa and particularly from south of the Sahara. But the change will have a much greater impact on Christian populations. As recently as 1900, Europe accounted for over two-thirds of the "Christian world," with North America a distant second and Africa barely on the map. By 2050, by far the largest share of the world's Christians will be found in Africa, which should have a billion or more believers. By that time about a third of the world's Christians will be African, and those African Christians will outnumber Europe's by more than two to one. The Christian world will have turned upside down.

We can argue at length over what those figures mean and what future forms of faith might look like, but the raw numbers are not going away.

2

WHO'S COUNTING CHINA?

Phenomenal Growth
in the Number of Christians

I was perilously close to becoming an agnostic—at least about certain statistics. Specifically, I really didn't know the data on Christians in China, and for a while I was not sure if anyone did. Only now, perhaps, do we have the glimmerings of an answer to one of the most pressing questions in global religion: just how many Chinese Christians are there?

This question matters enormously because of China's vast population—now over 1.3 billion—and its emerging role as a global superpower. If Christians make up even a sizable minority within that country, that could be a political fact of huge significance.

Some years ago, veteran journalist David Aikman suggested that China's Christian population was reaching critical mass and that Christianity would achieve cultural and political hegemony by 2030 or so. Writing in *First Things* last year, Catholic China-watcher Francesco Sisci agreed that "we are near a Constantinian moment for the Chinese Empire." If we could say confidently that China today had, say, 100 or 150 million Christian believers, that would also make the country one of the largest centers of the faith worldwide, with the potential of a still greater role in years to come.

But what can we actually say with confidence when honest and reliable authorities differ so widely on the basic numbers? Estimates of Christian numbers vary enormously, from 25 million or so to an incredible 200 million. If current estimates are so contested, then so are growth projections.

One of the most authoritative sources on

religious statistics is the World Christian Database, which offers invaluable reference materials on all parts of the world. On China, though, WCD figures are startlingly high (which does not necessarily make them wrong). According to this source, the country's Christians exploded from under a million in 1970 to around 120 million today (over 9 percent of the whole country), and that number will grow to 220 million by 2050. If correct, that would make the story of Chinese Christianity probably the most dramatic success story in modern religious history.

Other sources, however, place the Christian share of the population significantly lower. The minimum realistic figure is that of the Chinese government itself, which to say the least has no vested interest in exaggerating the tally of religious believers. The government publicly admits to the figure of 20 million for Catholics and Protestants combined—1.5 percent of all Chinese. Beyond those, of course, there are the unregistered Christian communities, the famous house churches, and their numbers are a total mystery. The WCD suggests that there are 70 million house-church believers, others say 50 million, still others far less. Putting the various estimates together, the Pew Forum gives a Christian population of 4 or 5 percent; the CIA's World Factbook puts it at 3 or 4 percent. The differences may sound tiny, but we are dealing with a colossus—in China, just 1 percent of the population means an impressive 13 million souls.

The best evidence we now have comes from extensive opinion surveys undertaken over the past decade, material that is now being made available through a Templeton Foundation–supported project at Baylor University, led by Rodney Stark, Carson Mencken, and other scholars. At first sight, this evidence portrays Chinese Christianity as much more modest than in some recent accounts, with a mere 35 or 40 million adherents. However, the researchers stress that these numbers identify only those who are prepared to admit openly to Christian faith. Depending on the attitudes of zealous local officials, such an overt admission might be suicidally rash. Pew survey evidence also finds many additional Chinese who might not describe themselves overtly as Christian, but who are prepared to consider the existence of "God/Jesus"; perhaps these are converts en route to full belief.

Putting the Templeton and Pew materials together, we can reasonably place the number of Chinese Christians at around 65 to 70 million, or a little less than 5 percent of the population. That falls a good deal short of any vision of "converting China." Christians constitute just a small minority within that country, roughly comparable to the percentage of Muslims in Western European nations.

Even viewed in these somewhat reduced terms, though, the Chinese number still inspires awe. Those 65 or 70 million Christians outnumber the total population of major nations like France, Britain, or Italy. Put another way, China has almost as many Christians as it does members of the Communist Party. Moreover, the Christian figure represents a phenomenal growth from the five or so million who witnessed the communist takeover in 1949 and from the subsequent decades of massacre and persecution. If not quite a miracle, this is a profoundly impressive story.

3

THE THREE FACES
OF GUANYIN

Any tour of the modern world's Seven Religious
Wonders would include a stop on the southern
Chinese island of Hainan. Here since 2005 has
stood a colossal statue of Guanyin, the Buddhist
goddess of compassion. The figure astounds not
just by its sheer size—it is 354 feet high—but
by the mere fact of its creation: it was commis-
sioned and funded by a Chinese communist
government long bitterly opposed to religion of
every stripe. The statue of Guanyin is an object
lesson in the new China's radically changed atti-
tude to faith—but also a warning to Christians
who place their hopes in any future mass conversions in that vast country.

When Westerners study Chinese religion, inevitably they focus on the Christian story. They know about the horrible sufferings of Christians during the Cultural Revolution of the post-1966 decade and the surging national revival that began in the 1980s. Some estimates suggest that China today has over 100 million Christians, with projections of 150 or 200 million by 2050. Even if those figures are too high—and I believe they are—we are still dealing with an astonishing success story. Visions of national conversion don't seem farfetched.

Missing in such accounts, though, are China's other historic religions, which have also benefited from the milder official approach. Buddhism, Daoism, and Confucianism were equally suppressed during the horrific Mao Zedong years, when literally a million temples and shrines were smashed and vandalized. Since 1982, these religious systems have revived and even received official support. Many temples have been rebuilt, and new generations of devotees have become priests and monks. China is now officially the world's largest Buddhist nation.

Viewing the different faiths together helps us to make sense of the government's otherwise puzzling religious policies. After all, the country is still ruled by communists for whom power is the absolute imperative. It seems odd that the regime would tolerate the phenomenal growth of Christian churches if they posed the slightest threat of creating institutions and structures that might undermine the authority of the Communist Party. When Chinese leaders lifted the persecution of the churches, what was in it for them?

Actually, they stood to benefit in many ways. In the 1980s and 1990s, senior leaders came to believe that the faith could serve official ends. The churches encouraged values of thrift, hard work, enterprise, and mutual support, so Christians could be valuable allies in the process of rapid modernization. And it was far safer for Chinese people to express their spirituality in the churches than in eccentric fringe movements like Falun Gong.

When Christian numbers ran out of control—and more seriously, when Christianity made deep inroads into educated elites and even into the party itself—then it was time to apply the brakes. In earlier eras, such a reaction might have meant a flat-out declaration of renewed war against all religion. But naked repression fitted poorly with the country's new image. Instead, the leaders made determined efforts to support other faiths, partly to counterbalance Christianity, but also to exploit what those religions could offer to the causes of modernization and national security. If Christianity implies good work habits, then an alliance with the older faiths legitimizes the Chinese regime by rooting it in the country's ancient history and traditions.

Such a realignment appeals to traditional-minded Chinese who still retain old loyalties, however much they had pretended to forget them through the darkest years. If a religion is seen as subversive, though, as is the case with Buddhism in Tibet or Islam in Turkestan, then official attitudes remain harsh. All such decisions remain firmly political.

This brings us back to the statue of Guanyin,

whose location constitutes a powerful political statement. Guanyin has three faces—one face is turned inland to China, the other two gaze out over the South China Sea. According to official statements, she thus extends blessing and compassion not just over the Chinese motherland, but also over the wider world and the Chinese diaspora.

Viewed more cynically, Guanyin proclaims the strength and glory of Chinese culture over a maritime region that threatens to become one of the most desperately contested on the planet. Chinese demands for sovereignty over the South China Sea conflict with the claims of half a dozen other nations and directly challenge U.S. naval power. As so often in history, religion provides a symbolic assertion of national strategy.

Religion in China is tolerated as far as the state and party believe it to be useful—and no further. Any hopes for further Christian expansion have to take into account this political context.

4

THE CRYPTO-CHRISTIANS

*One of the World's Largest
Religious Groups*

For most American Christians, restraints on the open expression of religious loyalties normally involve situations in which believers might be seen as imposing their views on others—through evangelism in the workplace or school, perhaps. But in many parts of Africa and Asia, in societies dominated by other religions or by militant atheist regimes, Christians experience such negative pressure that they refrain from even admitting they are Christians. Millions survive as crypto-Christians.

Just how common these covert believers are is a mystery. In theory, hidden believers should be immune to study, as they would never break cover; the people who can be studied are only the less discreet. But we often do hear of crypto-Christians, and the stories are startling. According to the *World Christian Encyclopedia*, as of 2000 Syria's Christian population was fewer than 5 percent, but most observers think that number is far too low. And the true number has surely risen with the influx of Christian Iraqi refugees. A million semiclandestine Iraqi believers would raise the size of the Christian minority to at least 10 or 12 percent.

In India, some guess the number of crypto-Christians is 20 million. Worldwide, the crypto-Christian population runs well into the tens of millions. For what it's worth, the *World Christian Encyclopedia* speaks of 120 million hidden believers. If that figure is right, crypto-Christians would by themselves constitute one of the world's largest religious groups.

Although many of these believers are isolated individuals and families, some sizable com-

munities have demonstrated astonishing powers of survival. In the seventeenth century, the
Buddhist/Shinto nation of Japan annihilated
a Catholic missionary presence that seemed to
be on the verge of converting the nation. After
persecutions that killed tens of thousands—
even a suspicion of Christian loyalty could lead
to execution—the organized church presence
was destroyed by 1680. Yet many thousands
of "hidden Christians," *Kakure Kirishitan*,
somehow maintained their secret traditions in
remote fishing villages and island communities,
and they continue to this day.

This catacomb church strayed from mainstream Catholicism, and many of its practices
make it look like a Shinto sect: its eucharistic
elements are rice, fish, and sake. Its followers
once knew nothing of the wider church, believ-
ing themselves to be the world's only true Christians. The stunning 1997 documentary *Otaiya*
allows us to hear very old believers reciting
Catholic prayers that first came to the region
over 400 years ago—some recalled in church
Latin and sixteenth-century Portuguese.

Believers lovingly display a fragment of a silk robe once worn by one of the martyred European fathers. The film shows us the two last living members of the indigenous hereditary priesthood, both frail men in their nineties— the distant successors of St. Francis Xavier and the Jesuit pioneers.

Jesus reportedly warned his followers never to deny him publicly, lest he deny them at the Day of Judgment. Throughout the history of Christianity, though, conquests and revolutions have repeatedly led to persecutions and forced conversions, and at least some Christians have responded by maintaining a subterranean faith. When the Muslim Ottomans overran the Balkans and the Near East, many Christian believers publicly accepted Islam but continued to practice their true faith at night and in secret places. They became *Lino vamvakoi*: they were like a cloth in which cotton (*vamvaki*) was covered by linen (*lino*), so that they showed only one side at a time.

The phenomenon of crypto-Christianity is likely to become much more common in the coming decades. Defensive tactics are scarcely needed when the vast majority of Christians live in self-defined Christian nations, but they become acutely relevant when millions of believers live in deeply hostile environments, in societies that are (for instance) predominantly Muslim or Hindu.

That is especially likely in a global age, when the faith is spreading rapidly in Africa and Asia, powered by new forms of media and electronic communication. In turn, the rapid spread of Christianity inspires opposition from other established faiths and ideologies. In the worst cases, believers can survive only by practicing concealment and subterfuge, however they reconcile that behavior with the text of scripture. Whatever the prognosis, crypto-Christianity is an important—and evocative—part of the worldwide Christian story.

5

CHURCH–STATE DISCONNECT
Official Secularism

Even after a century of Christian expansion worldwide, Europe still matters immensely in the map of the faith. According to the *World Christian Database,* Europe—including Russia—has 580 million Christian believers, which is more than a quarter of the global total.

Though few of them realize it yet, a great many of these Christians are about to experience a far-reaching change in their legal, political, and cultural environment. Europeans who have long been familiar with established churches are soon going to find themselves living with a U.S.-style separation of church and state, enforced by powerful secular-minded courts.

This revolutionary change results from the process of European unification. What was in the 1960s the European Economic Community morphed rapidly into the European Community. Now there is the European Union, with a set of emerging federal institutions, and prominent among these is the European Court of Human Rights, based in Strasbourg, which has the power to judge and condemn the statutes and policies of individual nations. Suddenly, and with remarkably little discussion, Europe has acquired something like an overarching supreme court.

As in the United States, religious affairs are attracting judicial attention. Last year, the Court of Human Rights heard a complaint by Soile Lautsi, who felt that the display of crucifixes in Italian classrooms violated the secular principles by which she wished to raise her children.

The court agreed in a sweeping ruling that raised fundamental questions about countless aspects of ordinary life. Not only should crucifixes be kept out of classrooms, said the judges, but so should any signs that suggest the school environment "bore the stamp of a particular religion. This could be encouraging for religious pupils, but [it was] disturbing for pupils who practiced other religions or were atheists."

Religious freedom implies the freedom not to believe in any religion, the court said, and that means the right not to be confronted by "practices and symbols which expressed a belief," especially when these are associated with the state itself.

The *Lautsi* decision would not surprise Americans, but it is quite explosive in the European context. However secular Europeans seem to be, a majority still takes very seriously the notion of established churches. (France is passionately committed to *laïcité* and strict secularism, but it is in the minority.) In Sweden, for instance, a land that many academics take as a classic model of extreme secularization, governments still do things that would strike American observers as alarmingly theocratic.

Although church and state were formally separated in 2000, Sweden's list of public holidays includes Epiphany, Easter, Ascension, Whitsun/Pentecost, All Saints, and Christmas. The very secular Netherlands has a similar list, while Denmark adds Common Prayer Day.

Like many European countries, Sweden still levies a church tax. Though voluntary, it is collected by the public revenue service. Some 70 percent of citizens still pay this levy, which in effect constitutes membership dues in a church that is a symbol of national identity. Across Europe, church taxes represent big money. Germany collects some $12 billion annually, giving the country's churches a rock-solid financial foundation.

In other aspects of public life, too, religion is hard to miss. Not long ago, an English court attracted some transatlantic astonishment when it ruled on the troubled issue of who exactly qualified as a Jew. A decision on this matter was essential because England has a system of state-supported religious schools, which gives the government a strong interest in ensuring that denominations enforce their rules consistently and equitably.

On a less charged matter, English schools have no problem in accepting explicitly religious displays such as Nativity plays. (These need not be too sophisticated theologically: recall the film *Love Actually*, in which one little girl in a Christmas pageant plays the First Lobster.)

Europeans, in other words, know little of the separation of church and state. But *Lautsi* means that they might be about to learn. *Lautsi* ruled that people should not be placed in a position in which they would have to use "disproportionate effort and sacrifice" to avoid officially supported religious manifestations. Although the court did not have the power to enforce its policy directly—for instance, by banning crucifixes in schools—it could order substantial damages, and the threat of litigation would make it difficult for individual states to defend their policies in the long term. The *Lautsi* decision opens the way for a thorough purging of religious labels and institutions from education, from the calendar, and from much public symbolism.

Following the controversy over the Danish cartoons of Muhammad a few years ago, European intellectuals began an impassioned debate about the role of religion, with many expressing the sense that the Christian contribution had been severely undervalued. The latest moves toward official secularism promise to keep that discussion very much alive.

6

MIDEAST CHRISTIAN FEAR

A century ago, a wide-ranging *Catholic Encyclopedia* tried to give believers an alternative to secular reference works like the *Encyclopædia Britannica.* Now available online, the Catholic work offers wonderful browsing for anyone interested in Christian history or theology. But reading some of the entries on the Middle East is heartbreaking.

As recently as the start of the last century, Middle East cities celebrated since patristic times could be listed as thriving Christian centers. Denominational loyalties and hierarchies—that of the Greek Orthodox and the Melkites, the Assyrians, Jacobites, and Armenians, the Catholics and even the Protestant missionaries—were lovingly described in the *Encyclopædia*. Such accounts make for poignant reading now, when we know that many of these Christian communities were slaughtered or uprooted in the extraordinary violence of the decade after 1915. A million Armenians and Assyrians perished, and millions more Greeks were expelled from what became the nation of Turkey.

The religious cleansing did not sweep the whole region. Christians survived in strength in Egypt, Syria, Palestine, and Iraq. But the other communities could never forget the years of massacre, which profoundly shaped their later actions. In fact, we cannot understand the modern history of the Middle East without acknowledging those distinctively Christian politics. When we look at the recent upsurges in Syria, Egypt, and elsewhere, we repeatedly hear the distant echoes of the bloody events that occurred during and immediately after the First World War.

That war transformed the Middle East, creating a new structure of states and igniting new forces of Arab nationalism and Muslim reform. As Christians were among the better educated and more prosperous groups, they naturally played a major political role. But they had to strike a delicate balance. They were understandably nervous about the rise of Islamic movements, all the more so when Muslim birth rates were so much higher than their own. As the Christian minority shrank in size and influence, it faced an increasing likelihood of persecution by a Muslim majority—and conceivably something like a repetition of 1915. The question was: How could Christians help create a strong and independent Arab world without awakening the Islamic giant?

Christians responded by espousing movements that could gain mass popular appeal, while remaining strictly secular and religiously neutral. This was in no sense a cynical strategy; it simply made sense for Christians to lead their societies in secular directions. Christians were among the founders and most visible militants of the region's once-thriving leftist, socialist, and communist groups.

Others became enthusiastic patriots for secular nationalist causes, including pan-Arabism.
The pioneering theorist of modern Arab nationalism was the Damascus-born Orthodox Christian Constantin Zureiq. Another Christian son
of Damascus, Michel Aflaq, was cofounder of
the Ba'ath ("Renaissance") Party, which played
a pivotal role in the modern history of both
Iraq and Syria. Coptic Christians, meanwhile,
were enthusiastic supporters of Egypt's nationalist and secular Wafd Party.

By the 1950s, such Christian-founded
movements were offering idealistic followers
a heady mixture of socialism, secularism, and
nationalism that was all the more tempting as
Arab thinkers struggled to come to terms with
humiliating defeats at the hands of Israel. Pal-
estinian Christians like George Habash and
Nayef Hawatmeh emerged as the most stubborn and resourceful foes of the Zionist state
and the most effective guerrilla commanders.

Although nationalist and Ba'athist movements appealed to Muslims as well as Christians, they were most popular with minority

groups that stood to lose everything from an assertion of power by mainstream Sunni Islam. These movements appealed to Christians, but also to controversial Muslim groups such as Syria's Alawites. Syrian and Iraqi Ba'ath regimes suppressed Islamist movements with a brutality that is difficult to understand except as the response of minorities who desperately feared for their own fates should they ever lose their grip on state power. Even Saddam Hussein's Sunni clique took its secularism very seriously.

Since the late 1980s, secular regimes and movements in the Middle East have suffered repeated blows, and this trend has been cumulatively disastrous for Christian populations. Rapid demographic change combined with a global Islamist revival to fuel the success of potent movements such as Hamas and the Muslim Brotherhood, which eclipsed secularism. Meanwhile, Saddam's lunatic invasion of Kuwait in 1990 set the stage for the destruction of his regime and the expulsion or exile of most Iraqi Christians. It remains to be seen whether

Syria's minorities will suffer a comparable fate in the coming years.

The main mystery in this story is why Western Christians seem neither to know nor care about the catastrophe that has unfolded before them in the ancient heartlands of their faith.

7

BRICS OF FAITH

*Religion and the
Four Emerging Powers*

When the U.S. government imagines the global future, the term BRIC features prominently. The concept was created in 2001 when researchers at Goldman Sachs identified four critical emerging powers—Brazil, Russia, India, and China. By 2050, claimed these experts, the BRIC powers would be challenging the United States for worldwide economic supremacy. U.S. officials have taken this forecast very seriously. Hillary Clinton recently listed these four "major and emerging global powers" as vital partners in any future attempts to solve the world's problems.

The BRIC theory has political, strategic, and military implications, but it also raises intriguing questions about the world's religious future. The BRICs will be the scene of intense debates about faith and practice—about coexistence and rivalry between different faiths; about the proper relationship between religion and state power; and, conceivably, about the use of religious rhetoric to justify imperial expansion.

Brazil and Russia are deeply rooted in their Christian heritage. Brazil has one of the world's largest Christian populations, and the country has a flourishing tradition of confessional-based parties and ideologies. Judging the strength of Russian Christianity is a thorny business, with estimates for the number of Orthodox believers ranging from 20 to 80 percent of the population—anywhere from 30 million to 120 million faithful. Certainly the lower figure would be accurate in terms of committed church members or attenders, but even 70 years of homicidal secularism failed to eliminate a deep core of Christian belief in the Russian people. Since the fall of communism, the country has seen a stirring revival of monasticism, and some of the most ancient and cherished Christian landmarks have been restored. And as in Brazil, the old established church faces unsettling competition from upstart faiths, including charismatic Protestants and new sects. To combat this development, the Russian Orthodox Church has sought the aid of the increasingly authoritarian Russian state, which would be only too happy to invoke religion to justify state power. The great age of church–state politics—of Holy Russia, in fact—might not be entirely dead.

Very different issues arise in India and China, neither of which is likely to acquire a Christian majority any time in the foreseeable future. But both countries have substantial Christian populations. China has anywhere from 60 to 100 million Christians—more than any European country—and most observers forecast steady growth in years to come. And while nobody doubts that India will remain overwhelmingly Hindu, the country probably has 40 million Christians. In both countries Christians are influential, with a strong representation in booming sectors of the economy. In both, Christianity is associated with social and individual progress—with literacy, education, and social mobility.

Both in India and China, Christians have to live in ways quite different from anything that has been known in the West for many centuries. They are small minorities, living among much larger populations holding very different religious and political beliefs and having to negotiate the conditions of coexistence on a daily basis. Although neither persecution nor violence is common or inevitable, such threats can break out with minimal provocation. While states normally exercise tolerance, that fact cannot be assumed.

Although the Asian BRICs are not going to "go Christian," at least not in our lifetimes, religion could yet play a key political role. However different their religious histories, Russia and China share some common political and imperial views. Both countries aspire to control a vast sphere of influence beyond their national borders, and in both cases they can justify such outreach by claiming to protect their "own people."

Many Russians have never accepted the loss of the former Soviet republics in Central Asia—the "-stans," where millions of Europeans of Christian heritage now live as minorities among mainly Muslim populations. The current Russian government has already been accused of wishing to restore the old Soviet Union. It would not be hard to imagine a future regime expanding its power into Central Asia and justifying its move as a way of protecting fellow Christians.

China too could well see a similar version of religious politics. Tens of millions of ethnic Chinese live around the Pacific Rim, where many have become enthusiastically Christian. This ethnic-religious presence creates tensions with mainly Muslim societies in countries like Indonesia and Malaysia, where popular violence has erupted. Might a future Chinese government cite the need to protect overseas Chinese Christians in order to justify a military expansion into Southeast Asia?

Whatever the political future holds, religious ideologies should matter greatly in a BRIC-dominated world.

8

NATIONS AT RISK

Fertile Ground for Persecution

It's the world's least desirable club: the league of failed and failing states. Every year, the Fund for Peace presents its list of the world's shakiest political entities. Qualifications for entry into the club include such factors such as demographic crisis, economic decline, and bloody intergroup conflict. A failed state is one that loses control of large parts of its territory and fails to provide rudimentary public services. State agencies become in effect criminal organizations, allied with gangs and terrorist factions in bloody battles over state property and natural resources. Gradually, the accumulation of disasters leads to the utter collapse of state authority and its replacement by private militias or warlords. Last year, unsurprisingly, Somalia led the pack of quasi states and nonstates.

Understanding the process of state disintegration is vital for anyone who cares about religion and the fate of fellow believers. Failed states are the troubled home of some of the world's largest populations of both Christians and Muslims, and the concentration of both faiths in dysfunctional and violent countries will grow apace in the coming decades. Billions of people will have to cope with settings utterly lacking in the fundamental protections and services that Euro-Americans take for granted.

African nations lead the way in state failure, with 11 of the top 20 cases in last year's listing. Six more are in east and south Asia; two in the Middle East; and just one—Haiti—in the Western Hemisphere. The fact that most of the candidates cluster in the tropics will matter immensely if climate change develops as predicted. This is the area most likely to be hit by global warming, with all that implies for spreading desertification and decreased access to water and food.

Of course, the problems facing these countries could improve, or perhaps the states will fragment into new political entities, and at least some of those could become stable and prosperous. But for the sake of argument let us assume that the world's present political map will keep roughly its present shape through the mid-century.

Because these countries continue to have the highest birth rates on the planet, their populations will make up an increasing share of the human race by mid-century, and will represent a major component of global migration. And largely because of these demographics, the failed and failing states will also be a critical element of the world's religious geography. By 2050, some 600 million Muslims—around a quarter of the world's total—will live in just three of these countries, namely, Pakistan, Bangladesh, and Nigeria.

The picture for Christians is almost as bleak. Of the nations that should by 2050 have the world's largest Christian communities, four are high on the "alert" list regarding current or imminent state failure. Taken together, Nigeria, Ethiopia, Uganda, and the Democratic Republic of the Congo could by that point have around 450 million Christians, almost as many as in the whole of Europe.

State collapse will be a central theme in the development of global religion. It will be a factor driving interfaith conflict. Failed states offer fertile environments for religious persecution: desperate people turn against minorities, while private armies offer the means to kill or expel large numbers. Sudan usually features high in catalogues of political failure.

A failed state also has a huge impact on everyday religious experience and practice. Of necessity, religious organizations have to take over most of the responsibilities and activities that a Westerner might expect to fall to government. Churches and mosques supply social services and, in many instances, take over legal and justice functions as well, providing arbitration of disputes and performing community policing. It is scarcely surprising that Islamic courts thrive in Somalia, Sudan, and parts of Pakistan where secular justice is only a vague rumor.

Among both Christians and Muslims, many dream, however fancifully, of full-fledged religious states that could suppress the anarchy and misery. Religious fundamentalism will not diminish until those societies develop strong states that can guarantee the supply of food, water, electricity, and sanitation.

Only when we in the Global North witness what happens when the state is taken out of the picture do we realize how much of what we regard as natural and inevitable in our religious traditions depends on the continued strength of political order and security.

9

MARTYRS IN THE FAMILY

What Seoul and Kampala Have in Common

What has Seoul to do with Kampala? In the 1980s, the term "Global South" gained currency as a means of describing those parts of the planet outside the advanced regions of Europe, North America, and Japan. Various writers, including myself, noted the dramatic rise of Christian numbers in that vast region.

The problem, of course, is that the whole concept of the Global South is outrageously broad, including as it does some very heavily developed regions, like South Korea, and many countries characterized by cataclysmic poverty and underdevelopment, such as the Congo. We should not use a term as vague as "Global South Christianity" without careful qualification. I tend to use it with the plural and speak of "Christianities."

Yet it is not ridiculous to compare churches in very dissimilar societies, provided they share significant features that distinguish them from the traditional Christian heartlands. In many African and Asian countries, for instance, churches are largely made up of Christians relatively new to the faith, either first- or second-generation converts, and that characteristic affects styles of worship and faith. Also, across the Global South, Christians live alongside numerous members of other faiths, possibly as small minority populations, so that they always have to bear in mind the risk of hostility from these neighbors. Christians bear with them a substantial cultural baggage from these other religions. In these ways, Christians in the newer churches operate on assumptions very different from believers in the United States or Germany.

Among these differences, I would stress another one that rarely receives the attention it deserves: African and Asian churches know the concept of martyrdom as a recent historical reality. In North America, congregations might commemorate martyrs through the dedications of their buildings or through liturgies. The martyrs' sacrifices are remembered in art (St. Andrew's cross, St. Catherine's wheel). Normally, though, the martyrs are associated with antiquity, with the world of headsmen and torturers, of the beasts of the Roman arena. Europe has produced plenty of Christian witnesses in modern times, especially under communist tyrannies, but speaking of martyrs normally evokes a world as distant from us as that of the church fathers.

Not so in the Global South. During the nineteenth century, Christian missions were often associated with the aggressive power of colonial empires, which meant that they were believed to pose a threat to native regimes. Some of these regimes were highly developed states in their own right, with the will and the means to defend themselves against suspect foreign influences. In consequence, the great age of imperial expansion was a dreadful time for Christian believers unlucky enough to live beyond the protection of British gunships or French armies.

Although rarely remembered by Western Christians, Asian and African believers suffered massacres on a vast scale during the nineteenth century. To take just the most outrageous examples: Korea's Buddhist-Confucian regime killed 8,000 Catholic Christians. Perhaps 100,000 perished in Buddhist Vietnam, including several hundred priests and nuns. By some accounts, even these holocausts were dwarfed by the mass killings under Madagascar's Queen Ranavalona. Hundreds more were slaughtered in Uganda in the 1880s. The Japanese occupations of the twentieth century added hideous new chapters to the stories of Asian believers.

These experiences—which are widely commemorated locally—have become the foundation on which later churches were built. You cannot comprehend Vietnamese Catholicism except in light of the basilica of La Vang, which commemorates both a Marian apparition and the great martyrdoms.

Such events are accessible to these believers in a way that stories of ancient martyrs are not for Americans. For a modern-day Vietnamese or Ugandan believer, the martyrs are people like them, living in a recognizable style and probably in a town close by. They might even be a direct ancestor, or that of a neighbor. The martyrs are familiar, if not actually family. This fact makes nonsense of any claim that Christianity is a foreign, Western religion imposed by colonialists. How could it be for them, when their great-grandfathers died for it?

Stories of conflict have a political impact. Even societies in which religious leaders strive for good interfaith relations have recollections of injuries suffered in the not-too-distant past—by the Buddhists of this temple or the Muslims of that town. Stories of persecution always underlie views of contemporary governments in ways that recall early Christians' ambivalent attitudes to secular power. However benevolent and democratic a regime may seem today, citizens know what its predecessors were like and what might well happen again. Memories of martyrdom shape faith and conduct. To that extent at least, churches in Seoul do have something in common with those of Kampala.

10

A SECULAR LATIN AMERICA?

In recent months, observers have remarked on the growing number of Americans who claim no religious affiliation (the "nones"), whose numbers are highest among the young. We can argue about just what these numbers mean, but possibly they do mark the beginning of a secularizing trend, a drift toward European conditions. Surprisingly perhaps, given our customary assumptions about Latin America, conditions in several Latin American nations mirror those in the United States. Increasingly these countries are developing a European coloring.

Several factors shape a country's religious outlook, and prosperity and the welfare net certainly play a role. A country's fertility rate also tells us a lot about attitudes toward religion. When a country develops economically, women are needed to enter the work force rather than remain in the home. Meanwhile, shifting religious values place less pressure on women to have large families. In turn, smaller families mean diminished links with religious structures—fewer children go through religious education or first communion classes. And couples who have decided to limit families tend to run up against church policies on issues of contraception and abortion. When sexuality is separated from conception and child-rearing, people are more open to nontraditional family structures, including gay unions. Whatever the causes, the European experience indicates that countries where the fertility rate falls well below replacement (2.1 children per woman) might be facing rapid secularization.

With that figure in mind, let's look at the countries of Latin America, and especially the most economically developed ones. A few decades ago, all had classic Third World population profiles and very large families. In the 1960s, for instance, Brazil's fertility rate hovered around 6 children per woman, alarming those who warned of a global population explosion. By 2012, though, Brazil's figure was 1.82, far below replacement level. Chile and Uruguay both record similar rates of 1.87.

Argentina is still above replacement, but the rate is falling fast. That's a social revolution in progress—as well as a gender revolution.

In religious terms, these countries present a complex picture, with strong evidence of a continuing passion for religion. Brazil is home to some spectacularly successful Pentecostal megachurches, which Catholic clergy seek to imitate in order to hold on to believers. New evangelical churches are also booming in the other Latin nations, to the point that Protestants claim to be living through a new Reformation.

At the same time, though, signs of secularization appear that would have been unthinkable not long ago. Nine percent of Brazilians now say they follow no religion, and the proportion of nones is much higher among those under 20. Uruguay emerges as the region's most secular country, with 40 percent having no religious affiliation.

Gay marriage offers a useful gauge of transformation. Uruguay passed a national civil union law in 2009 and seems on course to establish full marriage rights for gays. Brazil approved same-sex unions in 2004, with gay marriages following, subject to some local discretion. Argentina legalized same-sex marriage in 2010.

Abortion laws offer a more mixed picture. Uruguay permits abortions through the first trimester, while Brazil grants terminations to safeguard the life of the mother or in cases of rape. On both these test issues, Chile stands out as a conservative bastion, with a strict abortion law and no prospect of gay marriage rights. Otherwise, however, the region shows a major trend toward liberalizing morality on issues that both Protestant and Catholic churches hold dear. Over the coming decade, we will probably see liberal reforms triumphing in several more countries, with the churches doing little more than fighting rear-guard actions.

Obviously, Latin America is a vast and complex region with many widely differing societies, and no single model works across the whole continent. Uruguay is a radically secular outlier, while countries like Colombia remain staunchly conservative. Most significant, though, is the clear set of trends that we see in several of the most influential countries, especially Brazil. Although Brazil is a long way from European secularization, we can foresee the emergence of a triangular political setup involving Pentecostals, Catholics, and secularists and a constantly shifting balance of coalitions and alliances.

Of the three groups, the Catholics are undoubtedly the weakest, because the acute shortage of priests has so reduced the church's strength on the ground. Also, most of the new nones are former Catholics who abandon the church without making the transition to Pentecostal congregations. This is very bad news for a church that officially lists Brazil as one of the world's largest Catholic nations. In practice, many of those notional Catholics have already defected to other faiths—or to none.

We should certainly not start writing the obituary for Latino faith. But that faith will be taking quite surprising forms in the near future.

11

THE CASE FOR PROSPERITY

Prosperity can be a real problem. As new Christian churches have flourished in the non-Western world in recent decades, their conservative attitudes on theological and moral issues have caused some discomfort for liberal-minded Euro-Americans. In one specific area though, namely, the prosperity gospel, criticisms cross partisan boundaries. Even observers deeply sympathetic to the rising churches of Africa or Latin America are troubled by the astonishing success of U.S.-inspired megachurch preachers who present health, wealth, and material success as the essential promises of the Christian faith.

If that is indeed the core message of emerging Christianity, should we not be concerned about the future of the faith? Comprehending the prosperity gospel might be the most pressing task for anyone trying to study the changing shape of global Christianity.

In West Africa especially, it is hard to avoid churches with a strong prosperity theme. They find their most ostentatious expression in the wildly successful ministries of preachers like Ghana's Nicholas Duncan-Williams or Nigeria's David Oyedepo. Across Africa, prosperity teachings are central to the ubiquitous culture of revivals and miracle crusades, so much so that they overwhelm more traditional charismatic or Pentecostal doctrines. As distinguished scholars like Paul Gifford, J. Kwabena Asamoah-Gyadu, and David Maxwell have shown, the prosperity message has come to dominate the teaching of many new churches, which draw as much on American ideas of positive thinking and perky self-help manuals as on any familiar Christian theology.

In its most alarming manifestations—and the superstar ministries are by no means the worst offenders—prosperity teachings so exalt success as to pour scorn on the poor as stubborn infidels who have evidently refused to seek God's aid. In this version of the gospel, faith leads to tithing, and tithing ignites prosperity. A gratified Almighty will respond by opening the windows of heaven, pouring out blessings so rich that believers will not have room to store them all. You have to pay to play—and to win. And if the church's pastor follows a dazzlingly sumptuous lifestyle, that is just his way of exhibiting God's munificence to the world. These days, Elmer Gantry is a very familiar spiritual type around the world.

Anyone not alarmed by these trends is not paying attention.

The good news is that the prosperity message is nothing like the whole story. If we just take Africa, then Christians are hearing a great diversity of voices and opinions. While believers may well be hearing prosperity preachers, many will on other Sundays be attending more mainline churches with traditional theologies, groups very dubious indeed about prosperity teachings. Catholic, Anglican, Methodist, Lutheran, and other denominations all flourish alongside purely African churches rooted in those traditions. Most ordinary Christians, like other believers, tend not to absorb the entire message that they are taught in a particular church but draw selectively on what seems relevant to them. For all the excesses of some preachers, moreover, most prosperity churches also contribute practically to improving the material lot of their flocks. Their actions belie their simplistic message of "Just tithe, have faith, and stand back!" Matthew Ashimolowo, for instance, heads a potent transnational ministry headquartered in London, with a strong health-and-wealth component. His church teaches that poverty and unemployment are manifestations of sin, against which Christians must struggle. In practice, this means that the faithful should help other members of the congregation by giving them jobs and that the church sternly teaches habits of thrift and sobriety.

Most prosperity churches not only condemn poverty but teach invaluable ways of avoiding it, like actually saving up in order to buy material goods. Debt is a demon to be defeated. Few

communities in the world could fail to benefit from such a lesson, but it is vital for people
moving suddenly from a rural setting into an
overwhelming metropolis, with all the consum-
erist blandishments offered to the poor. In such
a setting, being a member of a church offers
life-saving access to social networks of mutual
aid and support, which teach essential survival
skills. Meanwhile, peer pressure helps believers
avoid the snares of substance abuse.

If the faithful do not actually receive blessings
too rich to count, at least their membership in a
church vastly enriches their life chances. David
Oyedepo has said that the prosperity promise
makes sense only in the context of enriching
the wider community far beyond the narrow
confines of the church.

Whatever their undoubted problems, prosperity churches do not represent a negation
of Christian faith. Controversies over their
teachings also raise one perennial question for
Christians of all persuasions: how seriously do
we believe that prayer can actually affect conditions in the material world?

READING GUIDE FOR PRAYER AND PRACTICE

Introduction

In Prayer

Most images of Jesus show a European face. By the 2050s most Christians will not have any European heritage. In your prayer today, picture the face of Jesus differently from what you are used to.

For Practice

Find a painting that shows Jesus with a non-European face. Put it up in your house or your altar. Share your thoughts and experiences.

1 / Religion by the Numbers: Demography Drives Changes

In Prayer

Reflect on this chapter, and bring your concerns and fears to the Lord.

For Practice
How are the faces in your own local church changing, or are they? Discuss what your community is doing to welcome new people. Next time you are in your church offer a sign of welcome to a person you don't know.

2 / Who's Counting China?
Phenomenal Growth in the Number
of Christians

In Prayer
Many people in China have suffered and do suffer for their faith; many have given their lives. Say a prayer for the martyrs and missionaries of China.

For Practice
Reflect and discuss the influence Christians have on the politics of your own country. Where do you see things going? What are the challenges?

3 / The Three Faces of Guanyin

In Prayer
Have you received anything good from a person who follows a religion other than Chris-

tianity? Hold that person up to God in your prayer today, and send them a blessing.

For Practice
Go to your trusted Christian news source, and read one article today on the life of Christians on another continent, for example, China, Syria, Nigeria.

4 / The Crypto-Christians: One of the World's Largest Religious Groups

In Prayer
Have you ever been in a social situation when you hid that you follow Jesus? Hold this memory up in prayer.

For Practice
Search for the story of a modern-day martyr who died for professing Christ. Read and share.

5 / Church–State Disconnnect: Official Secularism

In Prayer
Give thanks for the religious freedoms we often take for granted.

For Practice
Do you see any dangers for religious freedom to be limited in your country? Share and discuss.

6 / Mideast Christian Fear

In Prayer
Pray for all Christians in the Middle East.

For Practice
Discuss the message of this chapter, and discern one action that will help Middle Eastern Christians.

7 / BRICs of Faith:
Religion and the Four Emerging Powers

In Prayer
Reflect about the story of the coins in the Gospel of Mark 12:14–12:17.

For Practice
Have you followed a conflict between Christian beliefs and the power of the state in your country? How could you imagine yourself and your community responding to such conflicts?

8 / Nations at Risk:
Fertile Ground for Persecution

In Prayer
Hold up in gratitude the blessings you receive from your country.

For Practice
List three basic guarantees a state needs to advance its people so they can build businesses and live from their own work. Share and discuss.

9 / Martyrs in the Family:
What Seoul and Kampala Have in Common

In Prayer
Look up the Catholic calendar, and read the story and pray in the presence of a saint-martyr of this day.

For Practice
Current martyrdom is a foreign experience for American and European Christians but not so in other countries; share and discuss how the threat of martyrdom changes your lifestyle as a Christian?

10 / A Secular Latin America?

Do secular values such as the legalization of gay rights or abortion on demand support religious faith or do they deflect cultures on matters of religious faith?

In Prayer
Pray today especially for the Spanish-speaking community of your parish.

For Practice
Attend a mass in a Spanish-speaking immigrant community. What is your experience?

11 / The Case for Prosperity

In Prayer
Hold up to God your needs of this day.

For Practice
Share and discuss. Does the "prosperity gospel" affect your community? Does it seem part of the Biblical message, or if not, does it have any value to the Church at large?

ABOUT THE PUBLISHER

The CROSSROAD PUBLISHING COMPANY publishes CROSSROAD and HERDER & HERDER books. We offer a 200-year global family tradition of books on spiritual living and religious thought. We promote reading as a time-tested discipline for focus and understanding. We help authors shape, clarify, write, and effectively promote their ideas. We select, edit, and distribute books. With our expertise and passion we provide wholesome spiritual nourishment for heart, mind, and soul through the written word.